FIRESTARTER DEVOTIONAL

BY FORGE SPEAKERS

Firestarter Devotional

Published by Forge, 14485 East Evans Avenue,

Denver, Colorado 80014

ISBN 978-1-960455-03-1 (paperback)

Created by Forge.

Visit us online at www.forgeforward.org

In honor and appreciation of the many faithful Forge partners advancing the Kingdom and raising up More Kingdom Laborers every day, everywhere…

We pray you are encouraged and empowered by these devotionals to persevere in living as Laborers in the harvest fields. Each devotional has been compiled by the Forge Speakers from their unique experiences and written in their own voices.

CONTENTS

1

IMPACT THE WORLD FOR CHRIST

> "In the same way, let your light shine be-
> fore others, that they may see your good
> deeds and glorify your Father in heaven."

— MATTHEW 5:16

Do you want to make an impact for Christ? Hardwired within each of us is a desire to make our life count. We want to make a positive impact and a world of difference with the days we are given on Earth.

Here are 5 Ways to Impact the World for Christ and His Kingdom:

1. Love God - Make God your everything. Give Him full reign of your thoughts, motives, desires, hands, feet, voice, plans, wallet, relationships, and schedules. With God as the source of all you say, think, and do— the world around you will be impacted for God's Kingdom. The greatest gift you will ever give the world is your intimacy with God!

2. Love Others - A life of Kingdom impact calls us to see, stop, and spend time with people as the Holy Spirit leads. While loving others in such a way might seem a bit intimidating, it need not be. Stay up-close to God and ask Him to show you the next move.

3. Pray - Want to change the world? Pray. People who have been used by God in mighty ways attest that "Prayer is the work!" They knew they were not strong enough, smart enough, or capable enough to accomplish or overcome what they faced. They knew God was enough, however. Fill your days with ongoing conversation with God. Watch what happens as God leads, empowers, and encourages you!

4. Labor - Kingdom Laborers get things done! The words we will long to hear that day when we see Jesus face to face are not "well contemplated," or "well understood," or "well intended," but *"well done!"* Getting things done is the goal. How you get things done is up to you and Jesus! Be assured, Jesus will use all the ways He has uniquely made and gifted you for His Kingdom's sake.

5. Multiply - What would it look like if you equipped others who then began equipping others? Baton-pass everything you can, all the "spiritual wealth" you have received. Ask Jesus to point you to someone you can encourage, pray for, spur on, and train-up as a multiplying Kingdom Laborer.

Challenge: As you seek God, prayerfully process— are there any of the five aspects of a Kingdom-impact life mentioned above you might be missing or have room to grow in?

Prayer: God, prepare my heart to love and know You deeply. Let that love propel me into a life that reflects Your truth and Your love for others.

2

ARE YOU ASKING THE WRONG QUESTION?

> "If anyone is IN CHRIST, he is a new creation. The old has gone, the new has come."
>
> — 2 CORINTHIANS 5:17

Who am I? That is the question that circulates throughout our world today. We seek to find the answer by searching deep within ourselves, gaining social status, studying self-help books, and taking personality tests—all to no avail. Not only are we looking in all the wrong places, but I also believe we are asking the wrong question.

What would happen if we stopped asking "Who am I?" and began asking "Who is Jesus?" Paul tells us the key to understanding our identity in 2 Corinthians 5:17, "If anyone is IN CHRIST, he is a new creation. The old has gone, the new has come."

Jesus Christ specializes in making old things new. From the very beginning, God spoke and filled this new world with life. We can witness His ability to bring new life every year as the seasons change. God does not just do this with creation, He does it with people as well.

I recently witnessed the transformation of a young lady. She grew up hearing all the Bible stories and learning all the worship songs but did not want anything to do with Jesus. She attended a camp this summer, heard a Gospel message, and encountered the real living Jesus for herself. Someone asked her what the difference was between how she sang the worship songs now verses before when she did not believe in Jesus. She replied that the songs used to mean nothing to her—they were dead and empty. But now, she could hardly explain it. She could no longer listen to the same songs without weeping because of the greatness of God and all He had done for her. "I am not who I used to be," she said. "I am a new creation in Christ."

If your identity is found in Christ, you are a new creation in Jesus Christ. While we are sinful and needy, He is forgiving and filling. While we grow old and are dying, He brings new life that lasts forever. While we can be full of fear and doubt, He is confident and filled with peace and love. Jesus calls us to find our identity in Him and to trust in who He is.

Challenge: When tempted to ask, "Who am I," get into God's Word and remind yourself of who He is—the Great I Am, who makes all things new.

Prayer: Help me, Lord, to fix my eyes on who You are and to live as the new creation You have declared I am.

3
TRUE BELIEF

> "For God so loved the world that He gave His one and only Son, that whoever believes in Him will not perish but have eternal life."

— JOHN 3:16

What Bible verses do you know by heart? Have you memorized Scriptures? I wonder if John 3:16 is one of the verses you may have memorized?

I believe most of the world may have memorized John 3:16! It may be the most quoted Bible verse of all time. It is stamped on clothing, plastered on signs at sporting events, seen on bumper stickers, worn on jewelry, and can even be seen at times flying through the sky as ariel advertising planes circle large outdoor events.

To me, John 3:16 is the "worst verse" in the Bible. Not because it is not a true word from God, but because I think it is so misunderstood! People can easily quote it, but I do not believe people understand the fullness of the verse.

Some people believe in God's existence as a fact. They say, "I believe in God," the same way they might say, "I believe in Abraham Lincoln."

But this is not the kind of belief that saves us. And this is not the type of belief this verse is referencing. We know from the context of John 3:16 God wants us to believe in Him in a life-changing, so-filled-with-the-Spirit-you-might-explode-with-it, kind of way!

Challenge: Please open your Bible and read the context of John 3:16. Do you believe in God just in an intellectual sense or in a way that changes your life? There is a difference.

Prayer: God, shine Your light brightly on my heart. Reveal what is hidden there. May my faith in You transform my daily life for Your glory. Help me believe in You with all that I am.

4

CHARACTERISTICS OF A KINGDOM LABORER

" "If you love Me, keep my commands."

— JOHN 14:15

Have you ever wondered why a cup of tea tastes like, well . . . tea? After all, tea is 99% water. No chemistry degree required, even the youngest observer will conclude that tea tastes like tea because the water has soaked in the tea's flavor.

The same is true with Kingdom Laborers. Steeped in an up-close relationship with Jesus, Kingdom Laborers take on the life and character of Jesus. They begin to love as Jesus loves, think as He thinks, care as He cares, and act as He acts. Increasingly, Kingdom Laborers walk, talk, think, act, serve, give, and love like Jesus. In fact, the more time Laborers spend with Jesus, the more they resemble Him to the needing and watching world.

While Jesus has many valuable attributes His up-close followers take on, here are four main characteristics that mark a Kingdom Laborer:

1. Humility - Kingdom Laborers emulate daily what Jesus demonstrated in the most ultimate way on the cross. He considered the interest of others more highly than His own and sacrificed His own life so that we could have life. Kingdom Laborers humbly submit to God and love others with Jesus' mindset and willingness to act in such sacrificial ways.

2. Passion - Kingdom Laborers realize that passion calls them to ruthlessly trust and boldly obey Jesus in doing some crazy, out-of-the-box things for love's sake. Passionate Kingdom Laborers are contagious. As they live passionately for Jesus, others are deeply impacted.

3. Vision - Kingdom Laborers not only see the big picture of God's plan for the world, but they also increasingly see what God sees in their daily activities, conversations, and surroundings. Vision-filled Kingdom Laborers walk attuned and in-sync with God's purposes and loving ways. As they see and respond to God's work and plan around them, the world will see Jesus too.

4. Faith - Kingdom Laborers are growing and stretching, because they continue to move out of their own comfort zone and into a life of continual trust and obedience to God. Faith-filled Kingdom Laborers will change the world, because they increasingly trust God to do through them what God alone can accomplish.

Challenge: Will you continue to "steep" yourself in an up-close, daily relationship with Jesus? As you do, your life will continue to reflect Jesus' life and character within you, and God will impact the world through you!

Prayer: God, will you help keep me humble and increase my passion, vision, and faith? I trust that You will do it!

5
EVERYDAY MOMENT PRAYERS

> "And pray in the Spirit on all occasions with all kinds of prayers and requests."
>
> — EPHESIANS 6:18

It took me a large part of my life to shake the religious notion that prayer was reserved for special times and special places. Churches, worship services, revivals, and retreats—those all seemed like the appropriate venues for prayer. When someone was in trouble, a meal was to be eaten, a loved one died, a friend needed healing, or a sin required confessing—those seemed like the times to pray. I did not understand the concept of praying to God throughout the day and in everyday moments.

Can I let you in on a secret? I have discovered the more time I spend with God in prayer, the more I realize He cares about every aspect and detail of my life. What is more, God wants me to know the details of His life, what He is up to in His Kingdom, and what is going on all around me. God wants me to enjoy the ice cream I am eating and talk to Him about it because God loves good things and wants me to love them too. God wants me to be aware of the person near me who is hurting because when they hurt, God hurts too. And maybe He wants me to whisper a word of encouragement to them on His behalf.

Everyday moments, wherever we find ourselves—those are the times and places God wants us to have conversation with Him. He loves to be brought in on the details of our lives. He knows them already but is waiting to share them with us.

Challenge: Practice talking to God throughout your day this week. Remember, you can talk to God about anything and everything! Write some of your conversations down and review them at the end of the week. See how many different things you talk to God about daily.

Prayer: Father God, help me learn to talk to You about anything and everything all the time. Thank you for wanting to have an ongoing conversation with me.

6

I SURRENDER ALL

> "Therefore, I urge you, brethren, by the mercies of God, to present your bodies as a living and holy sacrifice, acceptable to God, which is your spiritual act of worship."
>
> — ROMANS 12:1

Have you ever heard the song "I Surrender All" by Clay Crosse? If not, pull it up on your phone, and give it a listen.

It is a beautiful song, isn't it? He has a great voice, and the song is powerful. Music can touch our lives in powerful ways, and lyrics have a way of sticking with us for years and years.

What does it mean to surrender all to God? When I first heard this song, my response was to pray this prayer to Jesus: "Everything that I have is Yours. I do not care what anybody else thinks about me because I know You gave everything for me."

Did the song leave you praying anything specifically?

Do you ever feel like your sins or worries are chains in your life holding you down and stealing your joy? I can tell you right now the only way to be free from those chains is to surrender it all to Jesus. Are you ready to break the chains and let them go? Jesus can do that for you!

The enemy wants to keep us bound in chains, but there is freedom in full surrender to God. Do not wait a minute longer. God is ready and waiting for you!

Challenge: Have you surrendered everything to Jesus? What are the things that are holding you back? Will you release them all, and give them all to Jesus who paid the ultimate price for you? He loves you more than you can comprehend.

Prayer: Lord, everything I have is Yours. I do not care what anybody else thinks about me because I know You gave everything for me. Lord, take all my sin and wash me clean. I am yours.

7
EQUIPPED FOR MINISTRY

> "His divine power has given us every-
> thing we need for life and godliness."
>
> — 2 PETER 1:3

Have you ever felt ill-equipped or inadequate for something? I know I have!

When my second child was born, we discovered serious complications that required a life-saving surgery. On that day, he was transported to another hospital. We quickly packed up our belongings in the hospital room, but we could not find my wife's phone. After looking everywhere, I pulled out my laptop and used the "find my iPhone" feature. It appeared as if my wife's phone was just down the hallway. As I looked up, the doorway read: "Soiled Linens."

As I stood alone at 4:30 in the morning, looking at a Goliath-sized collection of soiled linen bags, I certainly did not feel equipped with the right protocol, proper protective clothing, enough sleep, patience, or the gag reflex to face the task at hand. But I muttered a prayer asking for God's help and dove into the mess. After some time, with God's help, I found my wife's phone wrapped up in the bed sheets on which she had given birth.

Maybe you have a story or two of times you have felt ill-equipped to face the "giant" in front of you. The good news is, when it comes to what matters most, God does not leave us to our own shortcomings. He provides everything we need!

Jesus declared what matters most is to love God and love others. It is this kind of lifestyle that will advance His Kingdom every day, everywhere! He gives us the power to do this very thing: According to 2 Peter 1:3, "His divine power has given us everything we need for life and godliness." Acts 1:8 proclaims, "you will receive power when the Holy Spirit comes upon you, and you will be my witnesses..." everywhere!

Ministry is not left to the gifted few, or to those on a stage with a microphone. It does not matter who you are, what your background is, or the mess you may face. God has equipped you for ministry. He has given you an opportunity to daily make an impact wherever you go... even in the soiled linens closet of a hospital.

Challenge: What is God calling you to do that you feel ill-equipped to handle? Ask God to give you courage, wisdom, and the power of the Holy Spirit; then go do it!

Prayer: God, I hear Your calling to ministry every day, everywhere, and I will answer it! I know when I am weak, Your strength is made perfect within me. All I lack, You provide. Therefore, I declare my surrender to You. I ask for Your Spirit to empower me, and I will step out in faith to obey you!

8

STARVING FOR THE FATHER'S AFFECTION

"The thief comes only to steal and kill and destroy. I came that they may have life and have it abundantly."

— JOHN 10:10

I read a study that was conducted in 1944 with 40 infants. The point was to see if babies could thrive only by having their basic physical needs met without any added affection. Twenty babies were simply changed, bathed, and fed with no additional contact, while the other twenty babies had the same care but were nurtured with affection by the caregiver. They stopped the research four months into a yearlong process because over half of the first group of babies lost their lives. However, the second group of babies who had been nurtured by their caregiver all lived.

While this is a horrendous study, I wonder, is it possible that many who are in church and who claim to follow Jesus are just as starved of the Father's affection? The great thing about becoming a believer in Jesus Christ is that you are adopted by a Father who loves you and places you into a growing family. Followers of Christ were never meant to just get their basic needs met and be isolated but are meant to receive ongoing love and warmth through intimate connection with God and His people.

In the book of Acts, we see that God's family grew as they spent time together. They read and discussed God's Word, prayed, and enjoyed having meals in each other's homes. But we also see encouragement, uniqueness, and a togetherness that only the Spirit of God can produce in a group of diverse people. As God pours out His affection on His kids, each one goes out and invites others to be a part of this growing and close-knit family.

Challenge: In what areas of your life are you living without God's love? Are you a son or daughter of God but living distantly from His people? Wherever you find yourself, rest assured God wants to pour His affection on you every day because He is a good Father who desires to give you the fullness of life!

Prayer: Lord, help me to know Your love for me. Will You grow my friendship with You and Your people?

9
BUILDING GOD'S KINGDOM

> "And Jesus came and said to them, 'All authority in heaven and on earth has been given to Me. Go therefore and make disciples of all nations, baptizing them in the name of the Father and of the Son and of the Holy Spirit, teaching them to observe all that I have commanded you. And behold, I am with you always, to the end of the age.'"
>
> — MATTHEW 28:18-20

Few of us will ever stand on a stage in front of thousands to proclaim Jesus. Few of us will ever become pastors of churches or traveling evangelists. The plain truth is, most of us will live lives off the stage and out of the spotlight.

Some have looked at this ordinary existence and concluded it is just not possible for ordinary lives to build God's Kingdom. But nothing could be further from the truth.

Jesus exemplifies both methods of ministry:

- He spoke to large crowds.
- He spoke to individuals in ordinary moments.

Jesus made it clear through His life, there is just as much legitimacy and importance through the work of the ordinary Christian life as there is to the work of those who stand on stages and proclaim to many. The Kingdom is built through both methods.

For most of us, if we wait for that "epic" moment to share Jesus with people, we will never contribute to building the Kingdom. On the other hand, if we make the most of every opportunity, whether it be over a cup of coffee, with a random stranger on the bus, or in some far away country, we will see God's Kingdom built.

Just today, I had two salesmen sitting in my living room, trying to sell me windows. During a lull in the conversation, I began to share a little of my story about how Jesus had transformed me from the inside out. One of the men, David, began to share his story with me, and he ended up deciding he would try out a church I recommended in his area of town. An ordinary conversation made special simply because *Jesus* was made more famous resulted in David being connected to a Body of Christ near his home.

The next time you are tempted to think you cannot play a part to build God's Kingdom, think again. God uses ordinary lives every day to build His Kingdom all over the world.

Challenge: Look for ways to build God's Kingdom in the ordinary moments of your life today.

Prayer: Lord, help me to live on mission with You. May I be all about building Your Kingdom and not my own.

10

WHERE'S YOUR MOJO?

> "Consider it pure joy, my brothers and sisters, whenever you face trials of many kinds, because you know that the testing of your faith produces perseverance. Let perseverance finish its work so that you may be mature and complete, not lacking anything."
>
> — JAMES 1:2-4

I heard a speaker recently talk about his "mojo." While I was initially perplexed, I quickly caught on. "Mojo," he explained, "is the culmination of a bunch of things going well all at the right time and in the same direction."

When we have our "mojo" going, we are happy and confident. All our faculties, skills, resources, and energy are fine-tuned and working together. I resonated with the speaker. I often feel a similar groove when life is clicking for me. Maybe you do too.

As I read the verses above, however, I am not too sure God is overly concerned with our "mojo." James seems to be saying joy and contentment in life have much more to do with our confidence in what God is maturing and completing in us through all circumstances—good and bad—rather than just when everything good and positive aligns. It looks like our real "mojo" is walking with and trusting the Master no matter the circumstances.

Challenge: Can you celebrate the messy and difficult things in life? What is the first thing that goes through your mind when the unpredictable and difficult happens? When something negative or undesirable happens this week, take a moment and pause. Intentionally pray to God and praise Him. Choose joy in that moment.

Prayer: Help me, Father, to walk with You and trust in You, come what may. Please produce in me the fruit of joy. Strengthen me and help me to praise you as I persevere through various trials in this life.

11

FINDING THE JOY OF LABORERSHIP

> "Whatever you do, work at it with all your heart, as working for the Lord"
>
> — COLOSSIANS 3:23

An eight-member crew finished the painstaking task of installing a new HVAC system in our fixer-upper home. The crew worked tirelessly for two long days. Though young in age, they completed the job with great diligence, skill, and . . . *joy*.

My wife and I were impressed and grateful for the team's work. At the end of the second day, we gathered the crew to say thank you with some cold drinks, fresh-baked treats, and words of commendation.

The crew smiled and seemed to really soak in the gratitude and care. Then the foreman said, "You don't know how much it means to hear your words. We live and work the way we do for one reason: to hear only positive comments at the end of the job." Something far beyond a paycheck motivated these men to work as hard as they did with the attitude they displayed.

What an agonizing endeavor Jesus took on. Can you even imagine the horrific weight of sin He shouldered; the loneliness and separation He experienced;

the intolerable physical and emotional pain He endured? And yet, Hebrews tells us that the "joy" of what was to come enabled Jesus to finish the work He began. Perhaps it was the joy of a "well-done" from the Father that helped Jesus persevere. Maybe the joy of knowing salvation's work would forever be complete kept Jesus pressing on. Perhaps seeing the joy freedom brings on faces such as yours and mine helped Jesus endure each crushing blow. Whatever was the fullness of "the joy set before Him," this we know: what enabled Jesus to keep enduring and laboring was His focus and desire to please God and benefit us. Quite simply, Jesus was motivated by real and unadulterated love—He knew the joy of laboring for a greater purpose. Such love keeps us doing the hard things (and even the agonizingly painful things) willingly, lovingly, and joyfully. With such love, the focus is not on how difficult or easy our work is but on how much of what we do will please and benefit the One for whom we are laboring.

Challenges: Do you find joy in laboring for the King? Ask God to start speaking to your heart about the impact He wants to make through you. Let your motivation be a desire to please God and benefit others.

Prayer: Father God, refresh my spirit so my work may be marked by joy! Holy Spirit, remind me that all I do is for Your glory and Kingdom.

12

GETTING USED TO GOD

> "I know your deeds, your hard work and your perseverance. I know that you cannot tolerate wicked people, that you have tested those who claim to be apostles but are not and have found them false. You have persevered and have endured hardships for My name and have not grown weary. Yet I hold this against you: You have forsaken the love you had at first."
>
> — REVELATION 2:2-4

Apathy. Comfort. These things can be big problems in our walk with Christ. As Kingdom Laborers, we need to be on guard. We can become apathetic and comfortable way too quickly. What did your love for God look like when you first met Him?

Think about a time you first met a good friend. It was exciting—you called and texted them all the time at first. But as time went by, you might have found yourself getting a little too comfortable or apathetic. Maybe you stopped putting so much effort in and thought, "Hey, we'll still be friends no matter how much work I put into our friendship!"

Sometimes we treat God this way. Our love for Him over time can grow cold. We start to grow comfortable and act like He is less than He is, so it is no big deal that we know the Creator of the Universe, right?

Wrong! Absolutely wrong! I mean, we get to know the Creator of the Universe as our *personal* Lord and Savior. How awesome is that brothers and sisters?

Challenge: Have you gotten used to God? God is radically in love with you and wants to pursue an ongoing, intimate relationship with you! What changes can you make to pursue Him more? How can you make Him your first love?

Prayer: Lord, please forgive me for the times when I have become apathetic about knowing You. You are my first love! Please fan the flame in me so it burns brightly moment by moment. Give me a new hunger and passion for you like never before.

13

HOW TO BUILD UP THE KINGDOM AS PARENTS

> "One generation shall commend Your works to another and shall declare Your mighty acts. On the glorious splendor of Your majesty, and on Your wondrous works, I will meditate. They shall speak of the might of Your awesome deeds, and I will declare Your greatness."
>
> — PSALM 145:4-6

One of the greatest ways we can build up the Kingdom of God as parents is to invest in our children. In some cases, we have been programed by society to believe the greatest Kingdom impact we can make is toward a corporate goal or a specific ministry position. I have been there. I had, and still have, lofty goals to build up the Kingdom of God through things like international humanitarian endeavors, ministry positions, and authoring books—all great things. But, in striving to achieve such things, I lost sight of the first ministry God set before me: my family.

Kingdom impact should never come at the expense of our children. Our "kid and Kingdom" investment will be multiplied many times over as our children learn to love Jesus and impact the world—one conversation, relationship, and endeavor at a time! Here are four ways to invest in your children to build the Kingdom:

1. Pray - One of the most powerful things you can do to build up the Kingdom of God is to pray for and with your children! Let them hear you declare prayers and promises over them. Make conversations with God a normal part of your family's routine and life!

2. Speak God's Truth - Speak truth and pray Scriptures over them. Declare Scriptures and promises for them. Speak words of hope and faith over them. Believe God for them. The world is tough, and there is an enemy who is real. Both have a way of tearing people down. Be a parent who builds your children up through Scripture.

3. Communicate - Be open and transparent with your children. Let them see some of the things you wrestle with (age appropriate, of course), and have conversations with them in real time as you navigate various situations and circumstances.

4. Teach - Teach your children through real life moments. Process what worked and what did not work. Children have the capacity to learn at mountain-moving levels. Life is a great teacher, and when God is involved, nothing is wasted!

Challenge: Dig in deep in your prayer life and claim the truths of the Bible over your children. Find a time this week to intentionally pray with your children, guiding them in a conversation with God.

Prayer: Father, help me leave an eternal legacy through Jesus Christ for my children and future generations. Help me pray for them, speak Your truth over them, communicate with them and teach them Your way.

14

INVITING JESUS INTO YOUR SADNESS

" "Jesus wept."

— JOHN 11:35

Why would God cry? That does not sound very tough. Yet the God who came into the world He created is so in love with the people He formed and so invested in humanity that when Lazarus died, Jesus wept big, salty tears. Yes, Jesus cried too.

Why? Because He wants you to know your tears and heartache are not signaling a lack of faith but revealing an honest reality that we live in a broken world. It is okay sometimes to not be okay. There will be times you may sing during pain and other moments where you express your hurt in a flood of emotions. There may be moments where all you can muster is a sigh or groan to the God who weeps with you in your pain. Rest assured, God understands, and He is there for you.

Invite Jesus into your sadness, whatever that may be or however that may look. Let Him invite you into His joy as you trust your mourning and sorrow is all wrapped up in His resurrection life. God cares so deeply for you. He does not want you going through anything alone. Talk to Him, and share your every emotion. He understands better than anyone.

Psalm 119:28 says, "My soul melts away for sorrow; strengthen me according to your word." Will you give the Lord the opportunity to strengthen you today?

Challenge: What areas are you holding back for fear of looking weak or faithless? Talk to God about it, and find a place where you can be open with Him.

Prayer: Father, thank you for inviting me to share ALL of me with You. I bring You my heartache and pain in our broken, fallen world. Help me to process my emotions with You, my Creator. You have promised to never leave me or forsake me. I trust you with everything.

15
THE MAIN THING

> "And you shall love the Lord your God with all your heart and with all your soul and with all your mind and with all your strength."
>
> — MARK 12:30

I was once given a bumper sticker that says: "The main thing is to keep the main thing the main thing."

So, what is your main thing? If you are a follower of Jesus, Scripture makes it clear what your main thing should be.

A teacher of the law once asked Jesus, "Of all the commandments, which is the most important?" He was essentially asking, "What is the main thing?" "'The most important one,' answered Jesus, 'is this: ...Love the Lord your God with all your heart and with all your soul and with all your mind and with all your strength.'" (Mark 12:28-31).

Loving God above all else is not just one of many important things. It is the main thing.

The problem is most of us do not live like it is the main thing. We have a natural tendency to make following Jesus a religion instead of a loving relationship. And if we are not careful, we make obeying His commands the main thing.

God spoke clearly to the Pharisees and warned them about doing things out of duty instead of love: "These people honor me with their lips, but their hearts are far from me. Their worship of me is made up of rules taught by men." (Isaiah 29:13 and Matthew 15:8).

God is not chastising the Pharisees in this passage for doing something bad—they were honoring God with their lips. That is a good thing. Instead, He was calling them out for forgetting about the main thing—loving God with all their hearts.

Clearly, good things can be bad when they are not motivated by the main thing. So, this is the heart of the matter: Right words and actions must flow out of a right heart.

Love is the greatest wellspring of motivation on Earth. Love gets a "want-to" going inside of us, and it becomes impossible to shut it off. It seeks expression, even when it requires great cost.

The most important goal we could ever set for our lives is loving God. It is the pure motivation from which we obey. It is the wellspring from which we live. It is the main thing.

Challenge: Take a look within. Are you motivated by duty or love?

Prayer: Lord, I repent for not keeping the main thing the main thing. You are my everything. May my motivation and life's purpose flow from my love for You.

16

EXERCISE YOUR FAITH

"I am reminded of your sincere faith, which first lived in your grandmother Lois and in your mother Eunice and, I am persuaded, now lives in you also."

— 2 TIMOTHY 1:5

Faith. We live with it daily and depend on it constantly, even when we are unaware of it. We all have faith. The question is, "Faith in what?" Kingdom Laborers learn to increasingly put their faith in God. They learn to listen to and trust Him beyond what they can see, control, or know in their own wisdom, strength, and sightline.

That kind of faith requires exercise, "trust training," if you will. As our faith and reliance on God grows, we have the opportunity (and responsibility) to help impact and increase the faith of others. When it comes to the next generation, Kingdom Laborers pay faith forward!

Here are 4 Ways to Exercise Your Faith and Impact the Next Generation:

1. Make faith a lifestyle, not an epic event. Faith is powerful enough to move mountains. Kingdom Laborers want to practice a daily lifestyle of loving God, loving people, and responding—however, whenever, and wherever the Holy Spirit leads.

2. Develop "Yes, Lord" patterns of obedience. Small "Yes, Lord" obedience leads to bigger "Yes, Lord" Kingdom assignments. With every "Yes," your trust and confidence in God grows.

3. Share faith stories—yours and others. Hearing other people's faith stories often encourages listeners to engage their own. Be intentional, share your faith story with others! Tell whoever will listen where God is leading you and how you are trusting Him as you go. Keep God the focus and hero of your sharing.

4. Pay faith forward by journeying with others. Why not invite the next generation to test-drive faith? That is what Jesus did. He invited the disciples to journey with Him in faith—to experience for themselves what God was up to in the world, and how they could be a part of it. Look for opportunities to pay faith forward by sharing your faith stories. Invite and invest in someone as God leads, and watch God grow their faith as they join you in yours!

Challenge: What is your next step in exercising faith and paying it forward?

Prayer: God, grow me in my faith and reliance on You. Help me to listen and trust You beyond what I can see, control, or know.

17
REVIVAL TO AWAKENING

> "The High and Exalted One... says this: 'I live in a high and holy place, and with the oppressed and lowly of spirit, to revive the spirit of the lowly and revive the heart of the oppressed.'"
>
> — ISAIAH 57:15

When news began to hit about the outpouring of God's Spirit at Asbury University in 2023, I also witnessed God working in new, fresh ways globally. And it got me thinking: *what does God have up His sleeve for Asbury and beyond*? The revival at Asbury began with a chapel message on the love of God and our need for repentance. Worship bled over after the service, continuing 24/7 for 16 days. Over 50,000 people attended to experience God through prayer, praise, testimony, and Scripture reading!

What if a worldwide awakening movement is at the core of God's heart? What if ordinary people could simply be set on fire and be sent out as His Laborers so revival pockets could fan a worldwide awakening into flame?

There was a whiteboard at the 2023 Asbury Revival where students wrote prayer requests. At the center of the board was the prayer request at the very heart of Jesus Himself—more Laborers (Matthew 9:38)!

I believe two types of people are crucial to fanning revival into awakening: Itinerants and Laborers.

Throughout Scripture and history, we see itinerant evangelists spreading God's message from place to place as revival spreads! That is why Forge sends out itinerant speakers, following the model of Jesus and proclaiming Him from place to place!

But revival never ends with the preacher. Success of the movement always lies in the hands of the ordinary life. Even in Acts, the message spread from house to house, day by day—not through church leaders but through everyday people (Acts 8:4). And the same is true in history.

Challenge: As everyday people, how can we participate in revival and awakening?

1. PRAY! Before he had even begun his ministry, evangelist Billy Graham knelt on the floor in the same divots where John Wesley regularly prayed. He earnestly prayed, "Lord, would you do it again?" Clearly, God answered! May God answer our longing prayers for revival too!

2. Confess your sin and repent. This is always at the heart of revival movements!

3. Seek Jesus first. Not fame. Not ego. Not a better platform. Not better opportunities—just Jesus.

4. Share Jesus with those who do not know Him! Revival does not spread and become awakening unless people who do not know Him yet join what God is up to!

Prayer: Lord, will You do it again?

18

YOU'RE MAKING ME UNCOMFORTABLE

> "...David was dancing before the Lord with all his might, while he and all Israel were bringing up the ark of the Lord with shouts and the sound of trumpets."

> — 2 SAMUEL 6:15-16

Have you ever seen someone so filled with the Spirit while worshipping they started jumping up and down? How about somebody singing so loudly you could hear them five miles away? Joy and excitement have a way of bringing out the best in us!

Sometimes Christians look around and see someone filled with passion in worship, and they say, "Hey, would you settle down? You're turning people off." Because we are uncomfortable, we attempt to control someone else's personal expression of worship.

It is true you can show passion for God in a lot of ways, not just by jumping up and down. But do not forget worship in the Biblical Church was filled with joy, loud singing, shouts of praise and crazy dancing. It had to be absolutely contagious, don't you think? In the Scripture above, David was dancing with all of his might, shouting with praise and blasting trumpets!

That is not something we see often in church these days.

Sometimes we judge others' passion as a way to feel better about our own apathy, but according to the Bible, they are the normal ones! We all could use more passion, joy, and excitement in our lives as Kingdom Laborers!

Challenge: Do you sometimes find yourself judging others during worship? Ask God to help you. How can you show the passion and love you have for God in your own personal worship?

Prayer: Lord, I worship You completely. May I not hold back but give you all the praise due Your name. Help me give myself and others the freedom to worship You passionately.

19

THE DOMINO EFFECT

> "And Jesus called the twelve together and gave them power and authority…"
>
> — LUKE 9:1

Admit it. You feel your small acts of service are futile in light of the many needs around the world. How can you affect starvation, unclean water, poverty, trafficking, or even world evangelization? Consider this: if your small acts are futile, then so were the acts of Jesus.

We know that is not the case.

Jesus explained why the vast need in the world existed when He said, "The harvest is plentiful but the laborers are few" (Matthew 9:37). Yet, for the most part, Jesus did not try to reach the masses all at once. He always focused on the person directly in front of Him, performing single acts of service and changing one life at a time. He trusted in the "domino effect."

Think about it: Jesus influenced the whole world through twelve guys who were right in front of Him. It does not make sense, does it? Your small acts of service have a domino effect too. You can multiply His movement through every day, ordinary moments.

As He traveled from place to place, Jesus repeatedly reached out to and focused on the individual directly in front of Him. It does not seem like the most efficient way to reach the whole world, does it? Yet His approach proved to be powerful and effective as Kingdom Laborers multiplied.

Challenge: Consider the "ordinary" things you do on a typical day. Ask God to help you see how those ordinary acts of love can be transformed into extraordinary moments of impact. Is there something He has brought to your attention?

Prayer: Lord, help me to mirror You and what You did—loving the person right in front of me. I am trusting You to multiply the impact for Your glory.

20

HOW MANY SWORDS CAN YOU SWALLOW?

66 "Preach the word; be prepared in season and out of season..."

— 2 TIMOTHY 4:2-5

Dai Andrews swallows real swords every day. For over 20 years he has performed as an international sword swallower. He is very good. Dai holds the Guinness World Record for swallowing 15 swords at once!

And get this, Dai can swallow a 120-degree curved sword. If you are not sure what that curve looks like, imagine swallowing the crescent moon you see in the sky at night—only it is made of sharp steel. It is crazy stuff.

Even with all his expertise, years of perfecting his craft, and his world-renowned accolades, I was surprised to hear Dai say in a recent interview: "This is an art form, not a cheap party trick. No matter how accomplished you become, don't get smug . . . Once you think you know what you're doing, you take for granted that you're good. That's when you get distracted, and things go wrong."

Dai's words got me thinking about my comfortability with the Word of God. I wonder what it would be like if every single believer took his or her craft of consuming the Word of God as seriously as Dai Andrews does his sword swallowing? How seriously are you taking in the Word of God these days? Are you ready to share the Gospel in season and out of season?

Challenge: Practice reading God's Word this week with fresh eyes, an open mind, and great curiosity. Read as if you are reading the Bible for the very first time. What is God speaking to you?

Prayer: Lord, are there any parts of Scripture I am approaching too comfortably or casually? Renew in me a hunger and diligence for Your Word. Help me to be ready to present the Gospel at any moment.

21

DISCIPLING THE NEXT GENERATION

> "Train up a child in the way he should go, and when he is old, he will not depart from it."
>
> — PROVERBS 22:6

When it comes to discipling the next generation, you will find a litany of resources. I am not surprised. Especially considering the current cultural trends. Young people are leaving behind the Church and Christianity in droves.

After about a decade of youth ministry to kids on the "fringes," here are a few of my best learnings for discipling the next generation:

1. Connect students to Jesus. Everyone has a theory about why young people are leaving the Church in droves. Here is mine: they have not met the living Jesus. We need to connect students to Jesus, not just to the church, or to the youth ministry, or even ourselves.

2. Practice what you preach. Just like any other generation, the next generation is not going to let blatant hypocrisy slide. We need to think missionally. In a missional context, what you do is as important as what you say. Words without actions are empty.

3. Practice lifestyle Christian mentoring. Preaching has its place — I am a preacher, I know the value of it. If we want to see youth thrive, we need to do more than talk at them. We need to engage them in the conversation and show them how to follow Jesus.

4. Engage difficult questions and hard, Biblical truths: If you do not, who will? Should we proclaim the authority of the Word of God? Of course! Should we also teach them how to know why it is trustworthy? YES! Both are essential!

5. Do not abandon truth to make students comfortable. Students are hungry for truth. Proclaim God's Word, confident of its truth—always with love and respect, but always the whole truth. We have had students turn from sin-filled lifestyles as they hear truth. Stand on the truth of God's Word. Young people will thank you!

Challenge: Where is one place you interact and connect with the next generation? Reflect on how you can live out your relationship with God in that space and take a step this week to do just that.

Prayer: Lord, help me to see the next generation and genuinely engage them. Provide me with opportunities to share my faith, encourage others, and point them to You.

22

RAISE YOUR GAZE

> "So if you have been raised with Christ, seek the things above, where Christ is, seated at the right hand of God. Set your minds on things above, not on earthly things. For you died, and your life is hidden with Christ in God."

— COLOSSIANS 3:1-3

Are you okay to be you—the individual person God created you to be? He has a beautiful and unique purpose for your life.

You have unique traits and gifts, but sometimes all you can see are your personal struggles and imperfections. You desire to live in Christ's freedom, but perfection seems like an enemy. You love the life God has given you, yet there are times where you feel you have gotten the short end of the stick. One minute you feel the pleasure of God and the next your mistakes seem to ruin the experience.

The cross of Jesus Christ may expose our sin and imperfections, but at the same time, it also covers us with the forgiveness and righteousness of Jesus Christ. Remember this truth. May it be a gentle reminder. You are not only fearfully and wonderfully made by the God who knows you best (Psalm 139:14), but you are seated with Christ Himself!

Raise your gaze. Seek the things above. Look to Him who is seated at the right hand of God.

Challenge: In what area(s) do you need to be reminded that in Christ you are forgiven and free? Spend time talking to God about it today, and journal what He is speaking to you.

Prayer: Lord, help me fix my eyes on You and not on my struggles and imperfections. Help me trust Your righteousness covers all my sin, and Your victory is available to me! Raise my gaze to stay focused on You day by day and moment by moment.

23
WHEN SHOULD I LEAVE THE DINNER TABLE?

> "While Jesus was having dinner at Matthew's house, many tax collectors and sinners came and ate with Him and His disciples."
>
> — MATTHEW 9:10

Eating together is powerful because the meal table is the forum where ideas and values are naturally exchanged. No wonder it has been said some of the world's greatest ideas were written first on table napkins. Where else would people pull up close to each other and linger long enough to share their thoughts and feelings at a deep level?

Love expresses itself in natural ways at meal tables. Love shares more deeply at meal tables than at almost any other time of the day. Love lingers at meal tables.

In addition to being a connection place, the meal table is also the setting where family traditions and stories are passed from one generation to the next. Ask people where their family stories were shared, and they will point to those relaxed mealtimes—often during holidays—when no one was in a hurry to leave the table. They will speak with fond memories about the hours they spent laughing and talking. When their time together was over, they left with full stomachs and even fuller hearts.

I am probably not telling you anything you do not already know. You have likely experienced the relational power of these moments as well. But have you ever considered that mealtimes could be opportunities for ministry? Perhaps God would ask you to linger at the table a little longer to continue connecting with others on a deeper level. Life change can happen over a meal.

Challenge: Set an intentional mealtime with your family, spouse, neighbor, or friend. Honor God and love others in the midst of the conversation. If intentional meals with others are something new for you, consider setting one day a week aside to schedule a meal and great conversation.

Prayer: Lord, open my eyes to the every day, ordinary places where intentional ministry can take place—like meal tables. Use me as a catalyst to begin conversations that point others to You!

24
GOD'S DESIGN FOR THE HARD TIMES

> "Therefore, let those who suffer according to God's will entrust their souls to a faithful Creator while doing good."
>
> — 1 PETER 4:19

God confirmed to me that it was time to go—to leave my job and move, trusting Him. My wife was on the same page, and so, with three kids, we set out on an unknown adventure with God.

I remember the excitement of embarking on a Bible-like adventure. God was specific that we should not share our needs with anyone. We would need to wait and trust Him. There was no paid job offer. Simply trusting and waiting on the Lord for provision and direction.

In my comfort, I had forgotten following Jesus was at times extremely difficult. As time went on, I began to experience discouragement and depression. I began to wonder if God had forgotten about us or if we had done something wrong. I felt alone, abandoned by God, and without hope. This was the toughest season of my life.

But what if the difficult times we face are God inviting us to a closer relationship with Him? What if seasons of doubt are meant to lead us to more readily rely on God's truth? Maybe our emotionally bankrupt moments, the times we do not want to get out of bed, are the very things He is allowing—to lead us into a deeper, more vibrant faith in Christ.

Jesus said those who are in His will suffer in some form or fashion—we will be forced to face difficulty. Internal and external waves may come crashing over your heart, mind, and soul. But be encouraged by two things: you are not alone, and those waves are God's design to crash you into the Rock of Ages—Christ Himself.

In my personal difficulties, God began to change me internally. I no longer saw what was happening as God's disapproval or as failure on my part, but rather as God's refining, so we could enjoy a deeper and more vibrant relationship.

Challenge: Whatever you are going through, will you learn to entrust yourself to Jesus who also suffered? Will you trust God is faithful to not only begin a good work in you but also bring it to completion?

Prayer: God, help me to see my circumstances with eyes of faith. Help me to entrust all things to You— knowing You are working through my hardships to draw me closer to You.

25
A BUMPER CROP

"And Jesus went about all the cities and villages, teaching in their synagogues and preaching the Gospel of the Kingdom, and healing every disease and every infirmity. When He saw the crowds, He had compassion for them, because they were harassed and helpless, like sheep without a shepherd. Then He said to His disciples, 'The harvest is plentiful, but the Laborers are few; pray therefore the Lord of the harvest to send out Laborers into His harvest.'"

— MATTHEW 9:35-38

Imagine an apple orchard that spreads as far as your eye can see. Trees, loaded with ripe red apples, bend low, kissing the ground—"ripe for the pick'n" as some say. It is not just an "okay" crop or a "good" crop. No, this is a "bumper" crop—or as Jesus said it, "a plentiful harvest."

The picture Jesus painted for the disciples was a ripe and ready harvest—not of apples—but of people wanting more, needing more, ready for more. Life, *real* life, was right there for so many to receive and enjoy. Harvest-ready people—here, there, and every-where—were one step away from the God-centered, joyous life always meant for them. All that was needed was for God's people to share with them the life and invitation Jesus had to offer.

A plentiful harvest is not the issue. It is the workforce needed to gather the harvest. "The Laborers are few," Jesus says. Can you imagine being a farmer with a super-bountiful harvest only to discover you do not have enough help to gather it all in?

The shocking fact is, the harvesting is not complex and can be done by everyone! The word Jesus used with His disciples was "Laborer." A Laborer is a worker who rolls up his or her sleeves and gets things done. No specialized skills required, just a willing heart with active hands and feet. And yet, the Laborers—the willing workers—remain few.

The answer is not complicated. It is, however, costly enough that few choose it. After all, having an all-in active love for Jesus and others requires offering and trusting Jesus with our time, energy, resources, reputation, relationships, and so much more. Many speak of such love, but far too few activate it. Those who trust Jesus to supply whatever they need as they daily share His love and message discover the Kingdom Laboring life to be plentiful and well worth it . . . both for those they engage and for themselves.

Challenge: Jesus is looking for willing, roll-up-your-sleeves, no-special-skills-required people to get active in their everyday places of Kingdom harvest. Will you commit yourself to a life of daily Laboring for God's Kingdom?

Prayer: Jesus, I am all in. Give me eyes to see the harvest. Help me actively love You and people every day, everywhere.

26

UP-CLOSE ENCOUNTERS
WITH JESUS

66 "They said to the woman, 'It is no longer
because of what you said that we believe,
for we have heard for ourselves, and we
know that this is indeed the Savior of the
world.'"

— JOHN 4:42

Have you ever wondered how to become better
equipped for Kingdom work? Do you question if you
could really help others grow in Jesus? We have
countless resources at our disposal. We can listen to
sermons and podcasts from people all over the
world. We can take classes online or read numerous
books covering any Biblical topic you can think of.
While all those things are good and even recommended, they cannot take the place of our own up-
close encounters with Jesus.

Do you remember the first time you saw the ocean?
No matter how many pictures you had seen, or stories you had heard, nothing could compare to
walking the beach for the first time, feeling the sand
between your toes, hearing the roar of the waves,
smelling the salt water, seeing how vast the ocean is,

as if it has no end. Knowing about something is not the same as having first-hand experience.

In John 4:39-42, when others heard the woman at the well testify about her experience with Jesus, they believed her, but they sought Jesus out themselves. When they went from hearing about Him, to meeting Him and hearing Him directly, they truly believed Jesus to be the Savior of the world. Like the Samaritans, all the testimonies and resources at our disposal are designed to draw us to Jesus, creating a longing to personally encounter Him for ourselves.

We can live life, seeing Jesus and hearing about Him through the lives of others, or we can begin to spend time with Him, listening to Him ourselves, allowing Him to teach us, in firsthand encounters. He is a patient teacher and will equip us for every good work as we trust and obey.

Challenge: When is the last time you had an up-close encounter with Jesus? Be intentional to spend time this week getting to know Him.

Prayer: God, I long to know You more. May the ministry You do through me flow out of my up-close, intimate relationship with You.

27
HOW TO SHARE JESUS WITH UNBELIEVERS

> "And when Jesus came to the place, He looked up and said to him, 'Zacchaeus, hurry and come down, for I must stay at your house today.'"
>
> — LUKE 19:5

Growing up I was incredibly shy and awkward. Not exactly a recipe for making friends or being popular. I often felt invisible, almost like if I were to disappear no one would even notice or care.

I remember lunch and recess being the worst. It was the time of the day that most highlighted my loneliness. Sitting alone at lunch, quietly eating, I had no one to talk to. Then later, I would be walking around at recess quietly, with no one to play with. I remember feeling trapped by my own shyness. I wanted to make friends; I just did not know how. As a kid, I remember pleading in my thoughts with those who walked past my empty lunch table to "*Please*, just see me."

We often think sharing the love of Jesus is incredibly complicated. I think sharing the love of Jesus is actually rather simple, as simple as taking the time to see someone.

Just look at the story of Zacchaeus in Luke 19:1-6. It perfectly illustrates how Jesus loved:

> Jesus entered Jericho and made His way through the town. There was a man there named Zacchaeus. He was the chief tax collector in the region, and he had become very rich. He tried to get a look at Jesus, but he was too short to see over the crowd. So, he ran ahead and climbed a sycamore-fig tree beside the road… When Jesus came by, He looked up at Zacchaeus and called him by name. 'Zacchaeus!' He said, 'Quick, come down! I must be a guest in your home today.' Zacchaeus quickly climbed down and took Jesus to his house in great excitement and joy.

Take note of Jesus' actions. First, He saw Zacchaeus up in the tree. Not by accident—Jesus had to intentionally see. If we are going to learn how to share the love of Jesus, we need to intentionally see others.

Then, Jesus stopped. He did not just see Zacchaeus and keep going, He stopped and called out to him. How many of us have eyes to see people in need of the love of Jesus around us but just refuse to stop?

Jesus saw, stopped, and spent time with Zacchaeus. As a result, his life was forever changed (see Luke 19:8-10).

Challenge: If we are willing to open our eyes, slow down, and invest time in those around us, we may be amazed at how simple it becomes to share the love of Jesus. Who has God put in your path recently? How can you share God's love with them?

Prayer: Lord, help me to see those around me and intentionally stop and spend time with them.

28

NO BAND-AIDS REQUIRED

 "And He withdrew from them about a stone's throw, and knelt down and prayed..."

— LUKE 22:41

Jesus positioned Himself before the Father and knelt down to pray. I remember my father doing everything possible to prevent me from falling on my knees as a child to avoid bumps, scrapes, bruises and the need for princess and Elmo band-aids. There were times I did fall and scrape my knees and cry uncontrollably. My father had to remind me how he had warned me not to run. He just did not want to see his baby fall. He loved me so dearly.

Interestingly, now as an adult and child of God, I am realizing the importance of running to my Heavenly Father and falling on my knees before Him where no band-aids are required and where the tears are holy tears. I long to be in His presence. My desire is to be talking and praying with Him continually!

Luke 22:40-41 says, "And when He came to the place, He said to them, 'Pray that you may not enter into temptation.' And He withdrew from them about a stone's throw, and knelt down and prayed, saying, 'Father, if You are willing, remove this cup from Me. Nevertheless, not My will, but Yours, be done.'"

We can learn from Jesus and the posture He took in prayer here when life was hard. He kneeled and began to pray to seek the Father and His perfect will. Running to the Father and getting on our knees, like Jesus, positions us to do the same.

Challenge: As a Jesus follower, how often are you found kneeling physically before the Father? Has it been a while? When is the last time you declared, "Nevertheless, not my will, but Yours be done?" Perhaps it is time! Will you allow God the opportunity to speak to you as you kneel at His feet today?

Prayer: Father, align my heart with Yours, and help my posture to be one of humility that honors You continually. May my life be in full surrender to You and yielded to You and Your ways.

29
THE G.O.A.T

> "And now these three remain: faith, hope and love. But the greatest of these is love."
>
> — I CORINTHIANS 13:13

A mother recently shared with me about a season in her life when her son ran away from God. She would daily pray for things she believed were all good things for her son. She would ask God to give him a good day or to play well in sports. She was always looking for ways to pray for him. Then one day, she felt the Lord impress on her heart, "You're asking me for the wrong things."

She realized her prayers had been what she wanted for her son and not what God had wanted for her son. Her prayers quickly began to change. She started to pray, "God, help him to love You."

Prayers are powerful. It was not long before the Lord met with her son in his bedroom and saved him. Today, her son continues to faithfully love and follow Jesus, impacting others for the Kingdom. Love changes things, and God's love changes everything!

Jesus said love was the greatest of all these. Paul prayed we would know love. Scripture tells us God pours love out in our hearts through His Spirit, and it has compelled countless individuals to order their lives in such a way others might believe it.

Love drives what we do, and how we live. Love gives purpose and overflows to those around us.

Challenge: Is there anything dampening the flame of God's love in your heart or complicating its simplicity? Talk to God about it! Seek Him, and love Him with all your heart, soul, mind, and strength.

Prayer: Lord, fill me today with Your great love so Your fragrance spreads to others around me. Help me to love you well and love others.

30

GOD HAS GIVEN YOU A MISSION

> "You are a chosen race, a royal priesthood, a holy nation, a people for His own possession, that you may proclaim the excellencies of Him who called you out of darkness into His marvelous light."
>
> — 1 PETER 2:9

God has given us as the Church a mission, yet we have failed to accomplish the mission. How do I know this? Because we have: incredible access to Christian resources on demand for our spiritual growth, as many churches to choose from as Starbucks coffee shops, and paychecks with plenty of margin that could fund mission needs. In spite of all our tools, training and resources—we remain blind to the startling spiritual reality of the world:

• 95% of all Christians have never led someone to Christ (Greg Laurie).

• 70% of Christians have not shared with a stranger how to become a Christian in the past six months (Lifeway Research).

• 3.14 billion people (42.2 percent of the world population) live in unreached people groups (UPGs). UPGs are ethnolinguistic groups with little to no believers, resulting in no opportunity to hear the Gospel and no ability to sustain kingdom movement (The Traveling Team Statistics).

• There are 900 churches and 78,000 evangelical Christians for every one UPG (TTTS). Imagine what we could do if churches and believers teamed up to finish the mission! Even if only one out of every 900 churches sent one out of every 78,000 believers, we would engage every remaining UPG.

• For every $100,000 that Christians make, they give $1 toward reaching the unreached (TTTS).

It is time for Jesus' final command to become our first concern!

Maybe you have run from what God has called you to because you feel inadequate, ill equipped, unworthy, or imperfect. Maybe you feel you do not know enough, your past is too marred by sin, or you do not have the right words to say. Or maybe no one has ever told you about this grand mission of God, and you have somehow missed seeing the vast needs of the world. Maybe you have been straight-up lazy, living a selfish, passive life. Even still, the Creator of the universe has chosen you! If the Lord has chosen you, then nothing can stop you! It is time to let go of anything hindering you and time to embrace your purpose. Get up and start advancing God's kingdom —no matter the people, the place, or the cost.

Challenge: What has hindered you from fully joining God's mission? Read Genesis 12:3; Isaiah 49:6; Isaiah 56:6–8; Acts 9:15; and Ephesians 1:11–12.

Prayer: Father, thank you for choosing me for Your mission. Help me know how I can creatively and uniquely make Your final command my first concern.

MORE FORGE RESOURCES & OPPORTUNITIES

FORGE SPEAKERS & EVENTS
ForgeSpeakers.com

> Need someone to challenge your group to become passionate followers of Jesus who live with hearts on fire and lives on purpose? Book a Forge speaker for your next event!

FORGE EQUIPPING PROGRAMS for ALL AGES
ForgeTraining.org

> Forge Equipping is not summer camp and training events "as usual." Forge challenges and equips people of all ages to become unique, lifelong Kingdom laborers in their everyday places.

FORGE BOOKS & RESOURCES
ForgeResources.org

> Looking for a deeper relationship with God and practical ways to widen His Kingdom impact through your life? Forge has the resources you need.

THE FORGE APP
Essential Kingdom laboring tools right at your
fingertips:
TheForgeApp.org

JOIN THE MULTIPLYING MOVEMENT
Where everyday followers become Kingdom
multipliers:
MultiplyingMovements.com

FORGE VIDEO CONTENT
Subscribe to free video content:
Youtube.com/ForgeForward

FORGE PODCAST
FuelForTheHarvest.com

FORGE DAILY TEXTS
Scan the QR code or visit ForgeForward.org/Sparks
to join Spark of the Day
for one-sentence daily devotionals.

NEED PRAYER?
Email us at Prayer@ForgeForward.org.

CONTACT US
Forge
14485 E. Evans Ave., Denver, Colorado 80014
303.745.8191
info@forgefoward.org